Survivors

By the same author

The Nightowl's Dissection

Survivors

William Peskett

Secker & Warburg
London

First published in England 1980 by
Martin Secker & Warburg Limited
54 Poland Street, London W1V 3DF

Copyright © William Peskett 1980

Designed by Philip Mann

436 36710 6

Printed and bound in Great Britain by Clays Ltd, St Ives PLC

Acknowledgements

Poems in this collection have previously appeared in *Ambit, UCD Broadsheet, Encounter, Eureka, Fortnight, Fuse, QUB Gown Supplement, Honest Ulsterman, Irish Poets 1924 — 1974* (Pan Books), *Irish Press, Lines Review, Meridian, New Poetry, Outposts, PEN New Poems 1976 — 77* (Hutchinson), *Poetry Review, Prism International, Samphire, Transcript, Windless Orchard.*

Poems have also been broadcast on BBC2 TV *Closedown,* Radio Ulster *Saturday Supplement,* BBC Radio 3 *Poetry Now.*

Two pamphlets, *A Killing in the Grove* (1977) and *A More Suitable Terrain* (1978) have been published by Ulsterman Publications.

Contents

A Clearing in the Alps 9

Walking in the Agora 10

Given Sight 11

Dreams 12

City Scene 13

Summer Heat 14

From Belfast to Suffolk 15

Fenland 16

Mercy Killing 18

Kingfisher 19

Monster 20

Names for a Cat 21

Camping on Dunwich Cliff 23

Leaving 24

Casting Out 25

Crimes of Passion 26

At Home 28

Bamboo 29

Mouse 30

Ducklings 31

New Year in an Empty Church 32

Grime's Graves 33

First Love 34

The Colleen's Secret 35

Blisters 36

Underwear 37

Cri de Coeur 38

For Alexander Dubcek 39

Wasp 40

A Killing in the Grove 41

Coypu 42

Dogfish 43

An Astronaut Looks Down 44

The Box on the Beach 45

Winter Incident 46

Survivors 47

Rabbit 48

49 The Zoological Museum Revisited
50 Charles Darwin Comes to Eye
51 Entropy
52 Floods
53 Photographs
55 Earthworms
56 Flints

A Clearing in the Alps

Above the snow line,
above the conversation of the valley
we live precariously, as hermits,
seldom speaking each other's names.
We are surrounded by a litter
of building materials —
deadwood for the beams,
slabs of grey stone for a roof.
We light a fire to make us feel indoors.

The snow-fall section holds back
by the mountain roadside,
showing by moraine
its calendar of winter weather.
I know our footprints are in that wall,
a glove, a boot,
evidence of the marmot and the chamois.
All the angles we construct are made smooth;
the way home is covered.

It makes us try the harder.
Melting snow-drifts from the roof,
shovelling a dry path from the door
makes the comfort deeper.
We've won another winter —
after the thaw we find we're still in love.
We've made a clearing in the forest,
fought for ground between the rocks
to make our life distinct.

Walking in the Agora

Here is a template for a rooftile,
a yard to measure out
the style that men contrive.
And here are columns, tilted
from the temple
where their order made them sturdy
by solid mathematics.
Now light forces time through breaks
where waves of raiders
have stolen marble, razed the roof.

The shells in which we now reside
model our impressionable lives —
our attitude is measured out
by space, imprinted by the texture
of plan and elevation.
We take tea in a banker's house,
half-built, assumed
from lime pits miles across the plain.
Left by civilised men
the temples fall in natural array.

Given Sight

If blind, and given sight,
I'd be afraid to see you now,
painfully to develop and stretch
my film of theory to gravure
across your skin's paper.
Rubbing my eyes
I'd walk out of myself
as out of a barn
and douse my dreams with days full
of splintered light.

Living close within your sight
I'd touch you in bed
in the brilliant morning.
Kissing you down on the white
sheet's texture below the
window-pane, I'd discover in you,
as in the sun
that as well as giving warmth
you penetrate my sense
to give me light.

Dreams

In truth I cannot reach you.
Caged within my nerves
I pace narrow circuits
finding exit only
when my systems sleep.

Inside, I fumble with keys
and combinations which betray
no function from within.
I think that I must know my dreams
to see myself perform.

And if we could play them back
like tapes — we'd meet in limbo,
we'd integrate, know.
In apprehensive paradise
we'd fear we weren't ourselves.

City Scene

On one side a mirror-
windowed block
will woo me to approach.
As I dodge to see myself
a door is opened.
Out in the street I'd expect
to find myself the host —
instead quiet impostors
will take my sudden secrets.

Across the road a bar
might be open as usual,
its lounge blown out
and fenced on the pavement
as a book is pulled from the shelf.
A man says you can cut
the tongue from an ox
but never take the shine
from its eye.

Summer Heat

The busride into town,
the smoky busride back,
the mission down the years
suspends me mutely again
in different combinations
of the same stark people.

In work the jokes
and stories take me in,
accept me in a tense bosom,
a pubful of accents
divided into postal districts
by dark snugs.

Foreign students in the café
move easily — they've smelt
the flowers in pavement barrels,
missed the sweat of the city.
The pressure is immense.
Sitting silent makes me
somebody's enemy.

It must be made up, imagined
from romance and a solid reputation —
this heat can't be actual,
the tension underfoot,
the journalism,
the sensational unease.

Now something's going on:
in late afternoon the yellow car —
the one we are watching
completely alone
at the end of the street —
blows like a valve.

From Belfast to Suffolk

First the pleasures fire the heart —
sutures of oak and elm
divide acres of polyploid grasses
into skull plates
to civilise every corner of the country.
Driving from the Low House
we might pass a dozen churches,
towers that indicate
walking distance across the fields
set alight with beacons.

More honest than the view from innocence
where plumes of smoke along the skyline
describe another operation,
here, the factory workers of the earth
are burning stubble,
purifying the season.
Later, driving tractors in the dark
the sharp spot-light turns
a glistening edge of soil
in long tracks across the land.

The night-police don't scare me here.
Like the man who, in the end,
neglects his mother for his wife
a faithfulness supercedes
the pleasures of the moon.
This demilitarised home
protects me like the other —
its signpost names pronounceable,
its fields the map
in my head.

Fenland

We made a sort of life
between the eel island and the crane,
between the water
and the blows of the sky.
Balancing on stilts we stalked
our drowning cows like prey,
we slodged through mud
and skated meres.
These were the movements of necessity.
Arriving back on high land
our tales were of the largest carp,
our fingers clean and wrinkled.

When they cut the Fifteen Foot
and Forty Foot the flat landscape receded.
All that was familiar
has taken its reflection down the drain.
Now we pole-vault the cuts
from white soil to black soil.
Our skin has dried and blown away,
our damp customs desiccated.
The fowl we used to trap in a maze of nets
have waddled down from acres of sedge
to strict aquaducts, too fast
for the punts on which we lay, wet belly-down.

The black peat has shrunk back
and now the iron post they sank
into the deep clay has risen up to show
where farmer's feet tread powdery earth.
Refugees from the bog, we have resettled
on this artificial pasture,
precariously dry below the water's surface.
Now we're swamped by sudden floods —
our new wheeled vehicles
are cut off by a breech in the bank,
our new field gates swing open on to water.

The ague must be in our soft bones.
In another downpour
we make infusions of poppy tea
and trust the low contours of our lives
to the width of drains
and the new machinery of sluices.
At Denver, iron gates determine
the level of our inundation.
Tall towers on the open flat,
the races draw fresh water to the Wash.
Trees reflect their precarious roots.
Our car turns back at water's edge.

Mercy Killing

On the dark road, in a passing room of light
a half-crushed rabbit breaks the journey.
Dragging its dead legs
to the illuminated limit of our horror,
in the pure vision of surprise
it is caught in private agony,
all strength for reflex gone.

Later, in the Plough, irresponsibly we agreed
that if reactions weren't so quick
we should have hit the wounded rabbit
or stopped to kill it with a stone.
We can't assign the blame —
the rabbit's distant pain incalculable,
a tear stops wounded in the light of your eye.

Kingfisher

Today a kingfisher
is brought to me,
before, the common blackbird
and the thin-necked kestrel.
These beautiful casualties
are the liquor in the head of the land,
they take my breath away
like the candle in the belljar,
like the lover who, gasping,
devours my sighs.

Now I walk on any pavement,
in any square,
and underfoot believe
I feel great armies mobilise,
slow empires heave.
In a kiosk I might learn
that I'd be a fool to split
on the paramilitary.
For every sniper brought down
ten more fall to arms.

It's a one-man war
with no point winning battles.
No matter how many days we win,
in the end they'll come
to take our breath away —
I need no more
than this evidence of undertow,
quick spectrum in brown sedge,
the moving earth,
hovering.

Monster

This year again you may surface
to take breath
and disturb the triggers
in your cold and opaque room.

Blind men who watch for you
refuse to believe their ears
when you break the silence as an otter-school,
a family of hoaxes.

Canny with years,
your lesson is to lie low
like the soldier in the hay.
Finding us still here you sink again.

Names for a Cat

Feather-stripper, meat-cleaver,
fur-comber,
stalker of the dusk,
threatener of confidence,
quick shadow of the night,
warm weight in the night,
reflector of light,
lord of luxury and sultan of speed,
muscle mogul,
there's something
in your subtle economy
that evades the rigour of the lens,
some way that the fugitive,
unnamed, escapes the law.

In desperation I could fix
an enigmatic machine in a bottle
and inscribe it perhaps
with a number or a taxonomic name.
Prowling round a central explanation,
your truth skips closely
over every method.
I could lend you an identity to catch hold of —
that's the unrigorous method
of the desperate scientist, the chequecard holder,
AA Relay member, kidney donor,
the patient schoolteacher, the poet,
the modern man, the grown man with the cares
of rock music spilling from his head.

If they found out who I was
I'd be finished.
The insulation of a name
protects me from the powers
of the artful definer, the describer.
It keeps me out of the catalogue
and off the death-list.

All names misname you,
curvewinder, arch builder,
builder of comforts,
passionate rejecter,
man-watcher.
If I called your name, you'd open,
man-deceiver.

Camping on Dunwich Cliff

For David and Irene Gibbs

At the place of a single gravestone
the sea tumbles under the cliff
and washes gravel south.
The old port is under water,
like silt from under specks of gold
church foundations have been panned away.
Now the archaeology of the town lies in streets
beyond the beach's dropped horizon.

Inches of sandy turf calibrate our lives:
the distance from the edge
administers our ten-year lease —
enough to make safe our temporary efforts,
with gas and billy-can,
to survive the windy day.
In the evening we shelter in the pub.
Now secure, in a hundred years
we must be prepared to go hurriedly by the back door
and leave our camp-fire songs above the bay.

Leaving

Again I carry your case
to the bright door
and watch the car recede.
I reflect that the county,
as flat as a palm,
has no hill to make
the waving brief.

You trace your fortune north
round coloured fields as on a map.
To corner quickly
is the only sure farewell.
Inside, I prove the upstairs
windows have no advantage, turn
and let the empty house contain.

Casting Out

It should be enough
to drive you round the bend,
the way they pick themselves from your nerves
like shrill gulls on a hulk of carrion,
the way they hurl you from the crowd
with an attitude you've got to change.

On the street the distance
makes you think you are a stranger
but your naked face betrays you —
you're the identikit of the gaolbreaker,
the rapist. You stop at dark shop-windows
to check you've combed your hair.

The only way they see you is alone.
Without your lover
there's something quite unnatural
about the way you act,
drinking on your own,
walking in the burden of the rain.

Crimes of Passion

1. Exhibitionist

Your flesh too big and weak
for a man,
you thumb dead leaves
and wait for your delicate audience.

Like me, you have to unfurl
your life and find it
nubile, motherlovely —
but I could never believe

in the terrified child.
Appraised, you find release;
in the mirror of your tears
you watch yourself survive.

2. *Voyeur*

Frightened by the need for words
or touch, you would never
try to steal my woman
but would leave her

a distant shadow,
alive on my skin-thin blind.
But then I know your women
only by sight.

Knowing them to be naked
I can never say a word.
Relaxed by our pleasure,
remote, you commune.

At Home

Two cats sitting on the mat,
you're upstairs between the daydream
and the dark, picking stitches
from a difficult seam.
Outside, the wind has dropped.

Inside a flat perspective,
peace comes
when energy has diffused away
down the persistent gradient
between our muscle and our work.

I have to love you in a different way.
A weak stimulus; the tired response
gives no release.
Our metabolism peaks
in office hours.

When the day ends,
when our blood dulls,
the sugar thins the imagination.
The fire fails, in bed we turn
to switch the passion on.

Bamboo

Beneath this lawn somewhere
the bamboo rhizome works.
By the morning there will be
a three-inch spike
where we usually sit.

Splinters under the fingernails,
a laser at the crotch;
when the whole jaw swells
the dentist taps each note to find
one key that screams the tortured chord.

Digging out a dark wound
I find a complicated root.
By the pains of tying ropes
and slamming shut the kitchen door
a particular agony is brought to light.

Mouse

The noises that we make are quite predictable —
the mouse is so ill it can only judder
in its tiny pain.

You said it was so pretty and ran upstairs.
You must have heard the iron on the step,
the lifting of the dustbin lid.

And I was so shocked —
on my fingers the little shame of urine,
the silent bravery of blood.

Ducklings

The ducklings came too old and sure
to imprint like shadows on my walk.
I thought that I might raise them
in my own image
and find my own reflection
in the way they grew and grew.

Aghast, I hold my god-child from me
and feel her heartbeat mine.
Across the barrier I create
I hear her speak
for all her age
and cry for their release.

Struggling to keep vanity
from the monstrous step
I bed her down.
Starting simply
I turn to tend slow plants and raise
my farmyard pets against the day.

New Year in an Empty Church

For Michael and Sheila Gooch

Deserted by parishioners
who might have brought electricity or, piously, a stove,
for us the empty church
could only make the darkness cold.

Within the walls, shade leached from familiar names,
candles lit both pew and tomb.
In secular sanctuaries of light
we grouped to breathe a carol's tune.

That winter, I recall, we worried
that only heathens care
to illuminate and heat the space between
the graveyard and the field, the gospel and the prayer.

Now, in summer evening, in kissing grass
we return to catch a glow-worm,
to find that holding it can't douse its light,
to find its body, in the darkness, warm.

Grime's Graves

Here is a clearing dimpled
by the innocence of hard work,
silent hollows where the echoes
that might be heard of slaughtered deer
and barbaric squabbles over meat are still.

Here are the axes and gentle picks allowed by time,
a shadow technology of pulleys
to hoist flints from the ground,
a chalk phallus, a pregnant girl,
scrimshaws from a quiet life.

Like voyeurs of sinless lovemaking
we pay to ogle these few remains.
Behind a broken window
the bearded man talks slowly of vandals
and touches his finger to the flint-axe stigma.

First Love

In his bottom drawer
he's got a box full of clichés
with obsolete stamps —
she liked to keep him informed.

He doesn't know the half of it,
the other half he's got all wrong.
She says that love is gone,
this letter is the last.

In her next she says it isn't fair to hide
what's inside; that she's young and frail.
But she lures him reeling
through the terrors of love.

She takes his love and leaves it.
Years on, the letters read the same —
indelible ink that taunts his unfit age.
He puts it down to his negligible experience.

The Colleen's Secret

A colleen picks through darkened graves
for fresh earth, peaceful corpses dead nine days.

Returned to light, a body, cold and mute,
submits to surgery; incisions head to foot

describe a strip of pale and ugly skin,
a ribbon to entangle sleeping lovers in.

Now I'm the object of a colleen's love
I pray my letters and my kisses are enough

to soothe her breast, pray she couldn't tell
if, entangled, I awoke to break her spell.

Blisters

Tattooed with salty water,
my finger is marked by a pale cushion
against habitual contact.

This warning has persuaded me
it's best to avoid
and bravely miss your company.

In avoiding you I go to places
where we often meet: the town,
the stairway to heaven.

The lie of the chisel in my hand
is marked by blisters, burst, not enough
to prevent the pain of being touched beneath the skin.

Underwear

When the box arrived he was so proud
he told her to put them on straight away.
There was a row and talk about love
but in the end she conceded
the touch of the satin and the nylon lace,
the result of promised silk.
Fighting back the tears
she moved her limbs in the fantastic costume,
in a conventional way.

When all was quiet and his pride was gone
she left him on the bed
and carefully folded up the things.
Love, she thought, has elevated our view,
denying appetites that don't fit in the picture.
We've just moved in from the jungle,
covering our tracks.
Stopping in the bathroom to run the water
she stole a glance at the lover,
her cheeks wet with tears,
her red nipples spittle-wet.

Cri de Coeur

Imagine cutting your wrists
and, like puffs of smoke
from a paratrooper's heels,
bleeding in the bath
from your peripheral circulation.

It's the act of a man
not getting to the heart
of the matter:
cries echo within the tiled walls,
smoke signals in still water.

For Alexander Dubcek, August 1978

Too late, it was ten years
before we came to know
the man untying his hands
and the man with the newspaper
and the man falling over in the rush of spring.

Intoxicated by the liquor
that we drink like water
the man was heady with liberties.
Then dustbin lids smashed trance upon trance
as disbelief rolled in.

Too late, I try to say
that the light was inside his head,
that it could light the season to white heat.
I say that he must not let it dim.
How dark the dark is in the hollow.

Wasp

In dapper livery of threat
a nervous wasp invades my silence
and circles in a temper.

During quiet landings
I wonder what the wasp could need
in my flowerless, metric room.

Wasps don't want my company —
their feelers detail suspicious plans.
I read their soothing braille as blackmail.

An angry colonial in a strange domain,
the wasp exploits my land without respect.
Each dawdling skirmish is a tiny warning

to me to stay where I am.
All I have to say is, keep your proper distance,
insect, I'm as mean as you.

Not noticing the time, she hurries out.
With empty pockets she coyly navigates
to her box of nagging sisters.

A Killing in the Grove

In the grove, lime twigs
hold decoys down
while wave upon wave
of songbirds, clouds of song,
are fooled down from the sky.

The unhungry hunters
get their guns and break cover.
Dancing among the flowers
they might as easily shoot
each other's legs
or insects, or the sky.

The birds fall like ashes
in the grove. A last sharp turn
in their fluttering flight
and silent energy dissipates
from the meatless things.

Coypu

The coypu may riddle
your riverbanks
and crumble your land
with shafts of dusty light.
If fields are to collapse
it is to reveal beneath
a more suitable terrain.

Underneath this stream a marsh,
below this feeble crop
the strong smell of acorns.
Slowly the coypu peels a view
from the ecstatic level of the river.
The banks fall
to the landscape's climax.

Dogfish

Packs of dogfish cruise
the continental shelf.
Muscles flexing in white W's,
the perpetual swimmers
catch their cold breath to survive.

Their sandpaper camouflage
falls back on the seabed.
Concealed behind the reputations
of salmon and eel,
the dogfish turn tail to miss the net.

An Astronaut Looks Down

This is where we live,
where all paths cross
between invisible stars,
where the turning mass
pulls down all our paraphernalia,
where it pulls our blood down.
Under this hard canopy we make our effort to survive.

Like the silver of a fish chained to the miles of the ocean
we're captives and we're free;
when night closes in
we take diamond after diamond
in our teeth and smash the sky.
Weightlessness in our limbs
we break the orbit home.

The Box on the Beach

The box on the beach
contains so much energy
that when it explodes
the whiteness is intense enough
to make you think a hole had been torn in your sight.
Now, in the quiet, the turtles lose their sense
and climb from the bright atoll
into certain death.
Finely-trimmed gulls
squall out of the sky
while rabbits, still as prey,
watch the sun move across.
The weather has been disturbed.
The air, pushed out, is so thin
that you have to gasp for the satisfaction of breath.

In the confusion you imagine a shout,
much louder than you can make,
which is echoed across the plain
and washed like a loud tide into every ear.
As the door slams, the chattering

cuts dead.

You hear the children using words
to check they're speaking the right language.
You hear them asking for a definition of peace.
You hear their question growing old.

Winter Incident

In a metal hollow
beneath the cold drift
you stop and face each other
with the sudden problem of survival.

You can push yourself out of the car
and swim up through the snow.
On the surface you must roll up like a child
or the white wind will knock you down.

You can gamble on staying where you are,
counting your breaths
as they seep out through the wall,
numbering your numb limbs.

In the end, the effort that we make
is not enough.
Rescue comes too late.
Two men die beneath the snow.

Survivors

In a swamp of fleshy fishes
one survives
and the numbers
let him walk on land
and run another gauntlet.

At every step he takes,
the choices made
improve his chance.
At every new horizon
the struggle is the same.

Rabbit

In winter, in the daylight dark
you shoot a rabbit
on the solid ground.

The heat of living
thaws a tiny millimetre of epitaph
from the frost.

The rabbit's heart
beats a static branch of blood,
its lungs release their tree of air.

The Zoological Museum Revisited

For the class of '78

We look at two species of lungfish,
their skin, like a fat woman's leg, not quite smooth,
their aimless sine waves distorted out of depth
by the glass's strict security.

As we watch their fins, like tentacles on one,
thin humanoid stumps on the other,
I tell you that the fish are primitive
but not ancestral. In the cases, skeletons confirm.

It's what they told me to say. Now, after the dodo
and the dugong, the sail-backed reptile
and the golden mole, they have wired into articulation
the bones of a man. After the rabbit and the rat

we come to this case last. Did I make my lesson clear?
We are not heroes but survivors.
After the primates there is no easy exit —
by the door the lungfish wallow still.

Charles Darwin Comes to Eye

Darwin in Church Street

When he's observing me
the uneasiness sets in.
My every glance a snarl,
all smiles submission,
the true line of his sight
makes me twitchy.

Darwin in Castle Street

He's all right in his place,
battling bigots at the Union.
Singlemindedly he established
a new cage at the zoo and labelled it
Homo sapiens, but I stampede
when he tries to include me.

Darwin in Lowgate Street

The symptoms of animalism,
the helical message,
the limitations of flesh —
these are for me to study, not to own.
I get the human horrors to think
I'm subject to the biology of a finch.

Darwin in The Rookery

Darwin put those pious people in their place.
Eventually he corralled them
in his island paradigm.
Now by the gate he waits for me,
his meticulous arrows of evidence
glance off my shield of shame.

Entropy

Outside, the chaos
of the universe increases,
fingers of disorder intrude through pores
to snap a bond, confound your complexity.
The fight is to stay as you are,
on a ledge
above the ocean and the plain,
to delay the fall into sediment.

Strong walls deflect the storms
that in your house would tear
the structure apart;
breakers that would swamp
your building's frailty
weaken the barrage bit by bit —
at first the membranes that skin you in
can take the strain.

Inside, quick mechanisms
replace, one by one,
the dots that make your photograph.
Working in a jumble, your life becomes a struggle
to protect the neat array.
Between the pattern and the random specks
the skin divides.
The shroud becomes you.

Floods

That week we were almost surrounded
by floods — every road we took
led past a field-drain,
a broken culvert. From the peninsula
we drove a dozen miles just to get
to the end of the road.
Finally, I had to ford a stream
and allow torrents of water
into the castle of my car.

It was like descending
an open mountain
towards the fields of the plain,
my eye's reference became a map
and lost the successive views of the road.
If only years didn't follow
blindly one upon the other
but were charted like this in a stream
of clear obstacles and stepping-stones.

Blocked roads, diverticula,
lead off like tunnels
from a darkened shell.
Is it only the physical world
or, perhaps, the surety of experience
that allows the view
from the ascending eye?
A clear road, a string of puddles,
white water.

Photographs

You hold up your photograph;
I hold up my photograph
and in between
there's a plain,
a forest,
a swamp,
an ocean teeming with life
until it's thickened like soup.
Also there is
the survival of the fittest.

If we came out from behind
our loving faces
I'm afraid
we'd be at
each other's throats.
We've got hobbyhorses.
We each have
our own interests
to protect,
ruthless genes   •
to push.

If the love were genuine
I suppose it wouldn't work.
We'd be laid wide open
to pirates
and gigolos,
cheats and hawkers
who could con us
and cuckold us.
They could charm their way
between our opportune sheets
and steal our fatherhood!

It's the way
to keep the tensions balanced
between the bodies
in the crowd.
An altruistic-looking skin,
a selfish programme
in the cell:
The photograph hides
the mechanism,
the love conceals
the care.

Earthworms

I never thought I'd last this long —
past the part where I learnt
how to live
and into the part where I live.
Now the death of every pope,
every snowfall,
becomes an experience
denied to unsurvivors —
the man in the paper,
the sparrow on the road,
the ones who do not age.

On my lawn, surrounded
by a frosty light, cold,
the touch of grass like clothes,
a couple of earthworms stupidly copulate.
It's a matter of existence,
the motive contained within the fact.
Like an object in a drawer
the worms remain.
In the cold dawn
the invisible future
they confidently plan.

Flints

Thousands of the flints had been found —
palm-flat they became remarkable
at last in gravel piles,
in pods of trodden earth.
Later, through the sieves,
through the bone fragments came the ghosts of men.

Behind the pits and quarries
in the confusion of new faces
their heads turned these workers into idiots,
into chimpanzees or murder victims.
Their split skulls made them cannibals,
their geometry the missing link.

The flint knappers, knowing freedom,
hid their truth in simple living —
flints to the cave; bones to the hearth.
When our lives have got them guessing
they'll find our link and know
our overstatement like dissection.

Survivors is William Peskett's second book in the Secker & Warburg Poets series. At one level, it marks his move 'From Belfast to Suffolk' (the title of one of the poems), but more importantly it shows him coming to terms with the world of nature and the world of man with a new maturity. These supple, perceptive poems establish Peskett as one of the best younger poets.

William Peskett was born in 1952 and educated at the Royal Belfast Academical Institution and Christ's College, Cambridge, where he read zoology. He is married and now lives in Suffolk, where he is a biology schoolteacher. His first full-length collection of poetry, *The Nightowl's Dissection*, was published by Secker & Warburg in 1975.